Prepared For Her
The Journey From Good Man To Great Husband

By: Carrington Brown

Table of Contents

Preface

All successful projects begin with good planning. Whether you are building a house or building a relationship, the blueprint you have in place will determine the success and longevity of the masterpiece you desire to create. When discussing marriage, the term masterpiece is not regularly used to describe it although it defines it perfectly. The lack of connection is due to a large percentage of people not being provided with a true image of what marriage is supposed to look like. Since a young age, I always had a desire deep down to be happily married and raise kids in an environment that truthfully was better than the one I was raised in. It didn't take long for me to realize there were a process and necessary education needed to reach a point of being able to create and be a part of a healthy marriage.

On my road to meeting "the one," I came in contact with many "other ones." I don't say that from a place of disrespect, but more so from a place of them truly not being the one and at times attempting to force them to be the one. Through all of my relational experiences, I reached a point where I knew what I wanted but had no idea how to get it. This direction was provided to me one Wednesday night after a C2L bible study my junior year in college. After my weekly campus ministry hosted our bible study, many of us would hang around just kicking it. Singing, dancing, cracking jokes, just anything that we could do to grow together and embrace the time we had together. As I sat on a desk observing my teammate, Tevin, pop-lock at 275lbs, the president of the campus ministry got my attention and asked if I could step outside. As I walked to the door, I recollected my last 24 hours just to make sure I had done nothing crazy that may require a little correction.

After intense assessing, I was good. As I stepped out the door. Danielle looked at me and said, "I have a word for you, bro. God has shown me the desires of your heart and although the desires are good, one of your desires is a skip step." I paused and asked myself, "what in the world was a skip step?" Before I could even guess, she responded," A skip step is when you have a desire for a specific end goal or prize, but you want to avoid preparing for it." She then informed me that my skip step was related to being a husband. She expressed that although my desire to be a husband is pure and from God, in order for me to be ready for that responsibility, I would need to embrace the process that would prepare me for that responsibility.

She said that once I choose to submit to the process, I would not have to wait long to meet my wife. I gave Danielle a hug, expressed my gratitude for the message and walked across the street to my dorm room. I opened the door to my dorm, walked to my room, shut the door behind me and dropped to my knees in prayer. "Lord God, thank you so much for the desires that you have given me. I pray that today you begin the process of taking me through whatever I need to go through in order to be a great husband. Take away what needs to go and add what needs to be added so that in your perfect timing, I am who I need to be for the wife that you are designing for me. In your son Jesus Christ's name, I pray, AMEN!"

Chapter 1:

The Blueprint

That night I submitted myself to God's process and with this process came a lot of changes. I had to cut off relationships, be more intentional about sexual abstinence, spend more time in His word and even apologize to young ladies I had been intimate with for not treating them like His daughters. The assignment with the largest impact was renewing my mind as it came to marriage. All my life I had grown up around married people, but none provided me an example of what it looked like to do it in a healthy manner. The marriages in my environment would be filled with infidelity, pornography, masturbation, verbal abuse, physical abuse and every other type of dysfunction you could experience in a marriage. Because of this, I literally had to be brainwashed with truth, due to all of the filthiness that had filled my mind.

As I studied and observed healthy marriages, I grew to understand that being a husband is an honor. Not only is it an honor, but it is a privilege and also a reflection of the trust that God has in you. To be given the responsibility of loving and taking care of one of His children is not a simple mission by any means. Therefore, it should not and cannot be taken lightly. With my desire to create a masterpiece of a marriage, God had to give me a new blueprint and He began with the foundation. The new foundation He provided me was built on His word and specifically Ephesians 5:21-33 which says:

Ephesians 5:21-33 New International Version (NIV)

[21] Submit to one another out of reverence for Christ.

²² Wives, submit yourselves to your own husbands as you do to the Lord. ²³ For the husband is the head of the wife as Christ is the head of the church, his body, of which he is the Savior. ²⁴ Now as the church submits to Christ, so also wives should submit to their husbands in everything.

²⁵ Husbands, love your wives, just as Christ loved the church and gave himself up for her ²⁶ to make her holy, cleansing[a] her by the washing with water through the word, ²⁷ and to present her to himself as a radiant church, without stain or wrinkle or any other blemish, but holy and blameless. ²⁸ In this same way, husbands ought to love their wives as their own bodies. He who loves his wife loves himself. ²⁹ After all, no one ever hated their own body, but they feed and care for their body, just as Christ does the church— ³⁰ for we are members of his body. ³¹ "For this reason a man will leave his father and mother and be united to his wife, and the two will become one flesh."[b] ³² This is a profound mystery—but I am talking about Christ and the church. ³³ However,

each one of you also must love his wife as he loves himself, and the wife must respect her husband.

These scriptures destroyed many of my beliefs about marriage and provided me a new lens, a true lens of what it looks like to do marriage properly. As I spent time meditating on this scripture and assessing myself, I realized that a primary step in being prepared for marriage was gaining true understanding of these scriptures and aligning my beliefs about marriage with them. It is without question that these scriptures had a major impact on my growth and were a primary cause of me being transformed from a good man to a great husband.

Chapter 2:

Reciprocal Submission Glorifies God

Ephesians 5:21 Submit to one another out of reverence for Christ.

When the term *submission* comes up in a conversation, the women often get upset and the men usually realize they made a mistake. True submission is a blessing in marriage and creates an environment of trust and safety. The problem is that the society has skewed the term by redefining it as a man telling a woman to jump and her asking "how high?'" News flash, that is not submission, it's slavery.

The term submission is defined as "the readiness to conform to the authority or will of others." Now reading this definition could make you think that the example provided is correct, but you must look past the words and into the context of the scripture. The word says by us submitting to one another we do so out of reverence for God. Meaning, how you submit to your spouse expresses deep respect and honor to God. Now when we talk about submission in relationships there are a lot of complaints about the lack of willingness that women have to do it. If were being honest, women have every right to reject submission and willingly do so… in the wrong scenarios.

What is often overlooked is that at the core of a woman in a relationship is the desire to help her husband in his process of leading their family and becoming his best self. If this is true then as men, we have been asking the wrong question when our wives struggle with submission. The question is not, "why isn't my wife submitting?" The right question is, "Why Is my wife not submitting to me." I define submission in relationships as the willingness to align yourself with the expressed standards, directions, and expectations of your spouse due to their obedience to God. The key phrase is "*obedience to God*." From my experiences and observation, a woman has no issue submitting to a man that has fully committed themselves to her and submitted themselves to God. Therefore, you must ask yourself, "Have I, through my submission and obedience to God, shown myself as being the man that my wife can trust with her future and the future success of our family?" And be honest with yourself. If you are aware that you haven't made the best decisions in the past and haven't stayed connected to God then repent and move forward with a new level of obedience.

Making the necessary changes will create the environment where your wife will be comfortable submitting to you. With the focus constantly being on the woman to submit, I do not want you to miss that the verse says you are to "*submit to one another.*" This means that not only is your wife supposed to submit to you, but you as well are supposed to submit to your wife. Let's take it a step further by saying you are not only supposed to submit to your wife, but I believe that as men, we should submit first. Now I know that may sound like blasphemy, but this is confirmed through the primary responsibility of men being leadership. As a leader, you don't give demands and take a seat. You give the vision and walk it out as the example in front. By you submitting first to God and then to your wife, you are walking in your role as a leader, and planting the seeds that you desire to flourish in your wife and your marriage. Don't forget, God created Eve as a help meet. This means her foundational role in the relationship is to help you in meeting all goals, dreams and desires for the family vision that has been created. If you lack the willingness to submit to her, then you void yourself of the ability to receive wisdom that will aid in your family creating

God's vision for them. This decision to lead as a man positions your relationship to reflect the love that God has for His church and position your covenant to revere God as He deserves.

Key Points:

- Submission in marriage should be led by the husband and replicated by the wife.

- Your wife's level of submission depends on her comfort and ability to trust you to lead.

- Your obedience to Christ will create an environment in which your wife is comfortable submitting to you.

Chapter 3:

Be A Christin Her Life

Ephesians 5:22-24 [22] *Wives, submit*
yourselves to your own husbands as
you do to the Lord. [23] *For the husband*
is the head of the wife as Christ is
the head of the church, his body, of
which he is the Savior. [24] *Now as the*
church submits to Christ, so also wives
should submit to their husbands in
everything.

As a football player, getting new coaches was not a rare occurrence. After every football season, teams across the country return to their old team with new faces. Going into college, I, just like every other athlete, had the expectation of becoming an All-American and for the team to win a national championship. Also, like the majority of teams, this did not happen. In my first couple of seasons of college, my team won maybe seven games, which is totally unacceptable at any level. As the spring semester began my sophomore year, the team heard murmurs about our head coach being fired and a new coach coming in. The second week of the semester this information was confirmed. Our head coach called an emergency meeting and informed us he had been fired and in the coming weeks someone else would be brought on to replace him. About a month into this spring semester our new head coach held his introductory team meeting. He spoke a lot about a change in culture, new expectations, and preparing ourselves to be on a trajectory to win and it happened. Two years after the new coaching staff arrived, our school won the national championship which had not happened since 1972. The results that the team experienced truthfully weren't a surprise. The reason is because the team did what any team has to do to be successful: buy in. When a new head coach comes into a program it is their job to cast the vision for the team. The vision must then be bought in by coordinators, position coaches and then to the players for everyone to be on the same page. Once a team receives the vision and buys into the vision, a new level of success is often the result that follows.

When God chose for you to experience the covenant of marriage, He also gave it a mission, purpose, and vision. For you to create the proper vision for your covenant, you have only to go to God, request the vision, submit to the vision and share the vision with your spouse. In marriage, we as men have to recognize that God is our head coach. As our head coach, He has created a phenomenal vision for it and gave us the responsibility of passing it on to our wives. As we submit to the vision and work the vision, our wives will follow our lead and align with the vision.

In Ephesians 5:22-24, we are continuing the *submission* conversation with added qualities in being given the blueprint of what your submission to each other is to reflect. That is the submission between God and the church. It is the responsibility of the man to lead in submission. A man's submission to God provides the example of being led from a place of comfort, confidence and companionship. So truthfully, a husband must be the reflection of Christ in the life of his wife. Now, this doesn't mean you must be perfect, but it means that you have to be submitted. Doing so will express the trust and confidence you have in Christ and increase the trust and confidence she has in you. Knowing who to follow is an important factor in being a great leader. Therefore, the confidence in your wife towards you will not only increase because of the way you lead but also because of who you are allowing to lead you.

Key Points:

- God is our head coach, therefore as he gives us the vision we have to submit, align and pass it on to our wives.

- The submission in your marriage is to reflect the submission between Christ and the church.

- Your wife's comfort in submitting is not only about how you lead, but also who you are allowing to lead you.

Chapter 4:

Service Through Sacrifice

Ephesians 5:25-27 [25] *Husbands,*
love your wives, just as Christ loved
the church and gave himself up for
her [26] *to make her holy, cleansing*[a] *her*
by the washing with water through
the word, [27] *and to present her to*
himself as a radiant church, without
stain or wrinkle or any other blemish,
but holy and blameless.

A common question that I get from my wife is "Why are you so nice to me?" It's funny when she asks me, not because it's a joke of a question but more so because she asks as if there was an expectation for me not to be. This question is always answered in reminding her of who she knows me to be after all of our years together and confirming that because she is my wife, she gets my love and care on a higher level than anyone else. Growing up I was not provided with a large array of men or husbands that walked in step with Christ and His expectations. Even still, I experienced conversations with a few that truly left a lasting effect. I specifically recall a piece of advice given in a conversation with a gentleman about manhood. The advice given was that "As a man, it is your duty to inconvenience yourself for the convenience of women." This quote stuck with me initially because of how deep it sounded, but as I grew, I recognized how much this quote reflected the love and leadership exemplified by Christ.

In verse 25, husbands are directed to love their wives as Christ loves the church. The question that arises from this statement is "How did

Christ love the church?" In John 3:16 the answer to this question is provided in verbal and visual form. It explains that "For God so loved the world that he gave his one and only Son, that whoever believes in him shall not perish but have eternal life." The example of love provided to husbands was shown in a father's willingness to sacrifice His only son for the sake of someone else's life. This love is shown by a father choosing to not only inconvenience himself, but also inconvenience his son for the sake of others and a greater purpose.

As husbands, we must consistently inconvenience ourselves for the convenience of our wives in every area of our relationship. Rather it be a late-night store run, cooking and washing, or even providing a foot rub knowing you yourself need a full-body shiatsu massage yourself. Now let's be honest, it is rare to feel like sacrificing for your spouse always, but enduring the discomfort will represent to your wife not just the level of love for her but also the type of love that you have for her.

No matter what the situation, you have to get out of fully focusing on what you need and ask yourself, "how can I serve my wife to convenience her to obtain her needs."

Early on in the relationship with my wife, we both had the strange feeling this was not just another relationship. As time passed, we saw why through progressing as individuals, growing in intimacy through conversation, and the constant talk about marriage and its possibilities. Before I proposed, we attended pre-engagement counseling to determine if this was just feelings of infatuation or if this was transforming into true love that led to marriage. Our counseling sessions were very interesting to us. Not because of the amount of new conversations sparked or the secrets revealed, but because many questions and conversations that arose had already been discussed between us. I will not lie, I felt like we were definitely ahead of the game. Because of our personal preparation, the conversations were going very smoothly and we were breezing through very important topics.

Until one day an issue rose I truthfully was not trying to hear or even discuss.

Upon my wife and I meeting, I had a best friend of the opposite sex I had known for years. When we first met, we connected out of interest of a relationship on my end, but after spending a little while getting to know each other, the relationship landed in the friend zone and we both agreed that it was a great place for it to be. Until this session I had no idea that my wife had an issue with this friendship but she let me know on this day. She informed me that due to us being interested in each other at one point, she didn't feel comfortable with us being so close and having the relationship we had. Do note that my friend and I's relationship contained no flirting, no going out, no late-night calls or conversations or anything of the nature; but even with all of that, my wife still experienced discomfort. As I expressed my lack of appreciation for the conversation and defended my friendship, our counselor stepped in and made a statement that was simple yet profound.

Our counselor looked at me and said, "Carrington I understand that this friendship is platonic and that you have no desire for anything more than that. Even though that is where you are, you have no idea about the emotional state of your friend or if she personally desires for you all to be more than just friends." Receiving this information opened my eyes to possibilities I never considered and almost made me sick at the realization of what I had to do because of this. The next day I gave my friend a call and let her know the situation and that we would have to discontinue our friendship. I couldn't even explain to you the feeling this gave me, but I knew deep down it had to be done.

Now I know some of you may read this and think my wife was blowing this situation out of proportion, but as her husband, I would have to say you're wrong. Since I've met my wife, she has always been the type of person that is very proactive. She likes to solve problems before they even arise. The decision that my wife made to have this conversation and express her concern was because she wanted to proactively protect our relationship from the opportunity of being destroyed from the outside.

As a husband, you will be presented with many situations in which the right decision will be made not based on how you feel, but based on the answer to the question of "What matters the most?" Although my friend and I had a great relationship and served as each other's support system for many years, in the end I had to ask myself which is more important? Maintaining the relationship with my best friend or creating an environment of safety and value in my relationship with the woman I desired to spend the rest of my life with. With as difficult as this decision was, it was necessary that it be made. Not only to show my wife how much she mattered, but to also prepare for the future sacrifices that would need to be made for the benefit of my marriage.

Being a husband is not only about sacrifice but also about equipping and preparation. Verses

26 and 27 inform us ,we are to *make our wives holy, by washing her with the word and presenting her to Christ as holy and blameless.* As the leader, it is your duty and responsibility to cover your wife in prayer and prepare her for heaven through spiritual investing and biblical progression. Yes, you heard me right. The responsibility of your wife entering into the gates of heaven are not just on her, but also on you and your intentionality with growing in the word individually to be equipped to invest that wisdom in your relationship. So, understand that the conviction you have been experiencing from not consistently spending time with God has a bigger effect than just on your relationship with Him. It also affects the relationship that your wife will have with Him. It's your responsibility to prepare her for Christ. How have you been doing?

Key Points:

- It is your duty to inconvenience yourself for the convenience of your wife.

- The tough decisions in marriage must be made from the perspective of "What matters most?"

- The "Well Done" of your wife depends on the discipline and stewardship of you.

Chapter 5:

Love You First

Ephesians 5:28-30 [28] *In this same way, husbands ought to love their wives as their own bodies. He who loves his wife loves himself.* [29] *After all, no one ever hated their own body, but they feed and care for their body, just as Christ does the church—* [30] *for we are members of his body.*

When discussing the characteristics of love and relationships, it is impossible to end the conversation without touching on priorities. How you live your life expresses how you prioritize your life and how you prioritize your life expresses the type of relationship that you have with your life. As individuals, it has become a common theme to seek a relationship with someone else before you have healed the relationship with yourself. This tactic has a 100% failure rate and it makes sense because it's a sin.

In Matthew 22:36-40, a dialogue is sparked between Jesus and an expert in the law that results in people having clarity on what their top priorities should be. The expert in the law approached Jesus with the intent to test and trap him. This expert presents the question of "What is the greatest commandment," and Jesus responds by saying, "*Love the lord your God with all your heart, soul and mind.*" This means that as Christians, our decisions and thoughts should reflect God being our number one priority. He then says, "*And the second is like it, "Love your neighbor as yourself."*" This follow-up to His response gives us the next two priorities that are meant to be aligned right behind Christ. These two are yourself and others. In the world we live in, we often make the mistake of putting everyone before ourselves which is great because its showing humility and service. The challenge is that it's impossible to give what you don't have. To love your neighbor properly, it is necessary that you have the energy and means to do so. To have these means, you must prioritize yourself through self-care and rest to be fully prepared to love and serve on the level that Christ requires of us.

With this provided clarity about the prioritizing of our lives, there is still a concept hindering us in loving ourselves and others properly. The challenge is that to love yourself and others properly you must know what love is. For most people, the definition they have of love is founded in feelings rather than choice and commitment. For most people, their definition of love is sourced in the dysfunctional representatives provided in their parents and guardians. So, what is the solution, you might ask? The solution is beginning the journey of seeking understanding and healing through the word of God.

The foundation of the journey begins with seeking the answer to the questions of "What is love?" and "What does love look like? Because God is love, you can very well assume that the answer to these questions are found in Him. In the gospels of Matthew, Mark, Luke and John, we are provided with first-hand accounts of what love looks like in the life of Jesus. You will notice as you read that Jesus was caring, nurturing, disciplined, focused, empathetic and intentional about all things. With His expression of love towards individuals who we believe didn't even deserve it, you can conclude that love is not a feeling but rather a choice. A choice to commit to the well-being of someone unconditionally whether they deserve it or not. It is the willingness to sacrifice personal peace and comfort for the freedom of others. When walking out love, it is necessary to observe Jesus also because He was fully God and fully man. Which means He experienced the temptations, desires and negativity we face and still chose love. His life was not only confirmation but also affirmation that authentically walking in love is possible for us.

After observing Jesus through the Gospels, your next stop has to be 1Corinthians 13. In this chapter, we are provided with the foundational qualities that love embodies. It basically gives us the blueprint of love and literal characteristics we can point out whether or not we embody them.

1 Corinthians 13

13 If I speak in the tongues[a] of men or of angels, but do not have love, I am only a resounding gong or a clanging cymbal. [2] If I have the gift of prophecy and can fathom all mysteries and all knowledge, and if I have a faith that can move mountains, but do not have love, I am nothing. [3] If I give all I possess to the poor and give over my body to hardship that I may boast,[b] but do not have love, I gain nothing.

[4] Love is patient, love is kind. It does not envy, it does not boast, it is not proud. [5] It does not dishonor others, it is not self-seeking, it is not eas-

ily angered, it keeps no record of wrongs. [6] Love does not delight in evil but rejoices with the truth. [7] It always protects, always trusts, always hopes, always perseveres.

[8] Love never fails. But where there are prophecies, they will cease; where there are tongues, they will be stilled; where there is knowledge, it will pass away. [9] For we know in part and we prophesy in part, [10] but when completeness comes, what is in part disappears. [11] When I was a child, I talked like a child, I thought like a child, I reasoned like a child. When I became a man, I put the ways of childhood behind me. [12] For now we see only a reflection as in a mirror; then we shall see face to face. Now I know in part; then I shall know fully, even as I am fully known.

[13] And now these three remain: faith, hope and love. But the greatest of these is love.

To truly be equipped to walk in love, you must assess and determine which qualities you do not embody and create a plan of depositing these characteristics within yourself. This concept of love is so important that the first three verses are focused on informing us, you can be fully active in your gifts and be fully wasting your time if love is not the foundation. With verses four through seven we are given the foundational characteristics that define love. As expressed earlier in the chapter, prioritizing yourself has to happen before you can be what you are called to be for others. To get your self-love on track, you have to be transparent with where you are as it pertains to applying these qualities when dealing with yourself. You have to ask, "Am I kind to myself?" "Do I protect myself?" "Do I honor myself?" Your answers will reveal the parts of yourself that you need to work on to align your level of self-love to where it needs to be.

So why does all of this matter? The answer is simple. As a husband, your wife deserves the highest level of intimacy and love from you. Providing these experiences to her are impossible if your relationship with God isn't aligned or your relationship with yourself isn't healthy. Jesus was our tangible representation of love in action, therefore to love properly looks like embodying 1 Corinthians 13 toward yourself, your wife and others to follow.

Key Points:

- You can't fulfill the two greatest commandments if you don't love yourself properly.

- 1 Corinthians 13 provides you a blueprint of the qualities that make up love.

- Jesus was our tangible representation of love in action.

Chapter 6:

The Responsibility Is Yours!

(Ephesians 5:31) "For this reason a man will leave his father and mother and be united to his wife, and the two will become one flesh."

In the movie "Think Like a Man" Michael, played by Terrence J, had found himself connected with a woman he desired a future with. The problem is there was another woman in his life that had been his top priority since birth, his mother. All throughout the movie, his mother would contact him with a request and he would stop whatever he was doing to appease her. This was accepting and understanding until Candace, played by Regina Hall, found out that Michael had saved his mother under a different name so he could have conversations with his mother and not make Candace feel uncomfortable. This situation almost tore apart their relationship until Michael took action in a way that all men have to if they desire a serious relationship with someone else. He set boundaries. He went over to his mother's home and laid down the law. He explained to her that the changes in their relationship doesn't change the way he loves her or discounts the sacrifices she made for him. After this conversation with his mother, Michael headed over to the park where Candace's family was having a cookout. She had no expectation of Michael coming due to a scheduling conflict with his mother but was ecstatic about the fact that not only did he show up, but chose to stand on a table and expressed how she was the number one woman in his life. Because of these acts of implementing boundaries with his mother and openly expressing the priority of Candace in his life, the relationship continued in a healthier manner that led to marriage in the sequel.

In verse 31 it expresses that *the man will leave his father and mother in order to cleave with his wife.* With any change in relationship comes the necessity of new boundaries. When discussing marriage in connection with this verse, it is declared that the responsibility of setting new boundaries is not on your parents or your wife, it is on you. God gave the responsibility of men to do this because his decision to build a covenant with a woman changes the relationship. If you are not already aware, these new boundaries will not only help you and your wife grow together, but also protect your relationship from being torn apart. As a parent, we often have a biased perspective towards our children. Yes, we know they are not perfect, but we are the only ones that can express that. With the love that parents have for their children, one of the biggest mistakes you can make in marriage is taking the problems with your spouse to your parents. The reason is because if your parents are not matured, they will not only provide you advice that is beneficial for you and not your relationship, but this information shared could also skew how your parents see your wife forever.

The verse continues on to say that as men we are to *be united with our wife,* which means to be joined together for common purpose. Making the covenant of marriage has more responsibility than changing your Facebook relationship status and ending the annoying question of "when are you going to get married." When God ordained that you and your wife become one, He also assigned to you a problem in the world. The ability for you to solve it, however, depends upon you two truly uniting as a couple and becoming tunnel vision focused on completing the mission assigned to your marriage. Therefore, when you say "I, do", you are not only saying yes to covenant, but also to the calling of solving the problem assigned to your covenant.

Lesson:

- As the man, it is your responsibility to implement new boundaries in the relationship with your parents.

- Keeping your marital challenges in your marriage will help you avoid additional challenges.

- The determining factor of your marriage accomplishing the mission of it depends upon how united you and your wife become.

Chapter 7:

Three Pillars Of Manhood

When I think about life, I see it a lot like school. To be elevated to a new level, you must obtain the information and show you can apply it on your current level. As men, the desire to be a husband is great and to intentionally prepare for marriage is phenomenal. What you must understand though is that before you can be a great husband, you have to be a good man. Being a good man is primarily about understanding what the foundational principles are of being a man. There are many expectations and qualities we have to embody to thrive as a man. With all of these characteristics, they can be divided into one of three categories. These three categories are the foundational qualities to be mastered before truly being able to thrive in the role of a husband. These qualities are pastoring, providing and protecting.

As discussed in chapter 5, your relationship with God is the number one priority and the foundational relationship that all others will be built upon. As a man, by pursuing marriage you accept the responsibility of pastoring your household and being the example of Christ within it. As a single, seriously dating, or engaged man, you will be doing yourself and future family due diligence by building an intimate and authentic relationship with Christ before you say "I DO." By building this type of relationship before your covenant you position yourself to build your life and your marriage on the word of God. As a man, you have to be equipped to shepherd. As a man, you have to be equipped to intercede and pray over your house. As a man, you have to obtain an understanding of the value and power of fasting to implement it to open doors in the future. Note that preparing to pastor your house has less to do with perfection and more to do with progression. To walk in the full reflection of what God has called us to be takes time, which is why it is best to start building now rather than waiting until marriage.

When discussing provision, one of the most common mistakes of men is the limited perspective we have of this word. For majority of men, the word provide means going to work and bringing home the check. We have limited this expansive term to only pertain to financial provision when that is only one area that we are commanded and needed to provide in. As a man, you not only need to be positioned to provide financially, but you also must be equipped to provide physically, mentally, emotionally and spiritually. To be a physical provider means to not only be present, but to have a presence. It is not uncommon for children to grow up in households where their father is present, but the essence of him is nowhere to be found. As a man, you must not only be seen, but you must also be heard and felt. The spiritual aspect goes back to building the pastor within you. It pertains to investing in an authentic relationship with Jesus Christ in which you two become one and you are living a life that exudes His love through example and giving. Providing mentally is about obtaining the knowledge and wisdom needed to interact and converse on eclectic levels. As a mental provider, you must be able to connect with people's interests, discuss a vast array of topics and be able to add to any conversation that arises. Not only will this benefit you as a man, but it will also play a big role in you attracting the woman you desire to be with. No woman enjoys a boring and basic man therefore the more you expand yourself mentally, the more you can invest and provide mentally. To provide emotionally is less about being in touch with your emotions and more about your ability to listen. It is very difficult to provide what someone needs if you can't hear them. Often when we are in conversation, we find ourselves listening to respond rather than just listening. When you train yourself to listen, it allows you to help others to alter perspective if needed, but also allows you to give direction they can receive due to them recognizing you hear them. Although I expressed that providing emotionally is less about being in touch with your emotions, it is still valuable for you as a man to communicate transparently about what and how you feel. One of the most common complaints I receive from women in relationships is the challenge of communication with their spouse. For you to fully provide emotionally, you must leave behind any perspective that doesn't align with your spouse having an authentic desire to know how you feel. Specifically, I'm speaking of the notion that nobody cares about the emotions and feelings of men and that we need to just suck it up. King, you matter. Everything about you has value and is provided to you from God to fulfill a specific purpose. If you suffer from this perspective, you have to do what I did when I was still believing it. You have to give your spouse an opportunity to prove the belief wrong.

As men, there is a natural instinct within us to protect. Whether it's a woman, our kids or even our money. There is a switch in us that turns on when we believe that something valuable to us is being threatened. This quality is an asset and allows us to be on guard and ready to physically protect our valuables at all costs. What we don't want to do though is allow ourselves to only be trained in protecting something or someone physically. In relationships, a high value is placed on the ability to implement boundaries that protect the mental, emotional and spiritual of yourself and the individuals around you. I could touch on what it looks like to protect in theses specific categories, but the bible does that in Philippians 4:8. Philippians 4:8 says "*8 Finally, brothers, whatever is true, whatever is honorable, whatever is just, whatever is pure, whatever is lovely, whatever is commendable, if there is any excellence, if there is anything worthy of praise, think about these things.*" This verse provides us with the filter system that all things we are exposed to need to go through. If it doesn't make it through this filter then you do not need to be exposing yourself to it. That also applies to the valuable individuals you have in your life. To protect mentally, emotionally and spiritually is to force all things that will be exposed to your five senses to flow through this filter to assure that that they are conducive of being exposed to.

Lessons:

- The three pillars of manhood are Pastoring, Providing and Protecting.

- Providing is not just financial, but also physical, mental, emotional and spiritual.

- To protect is not just a physical act, but putting all things through the filter of Philippians 4:811.

Chapter 8:

Her Body Is A Temple

When my wife and I first met, she was almost a year into being sexually abstinent. I had been somewhat reverting to old ways due to some events that went on before our meeting. Although we were in different places with this discipline, both of us were advocates of sexual abstinence and truly wanted our relationship to embody this. The issue was we didn't discuss it until it was too late. This experience resulted in me being kicked out of her home and the next day receiving confirmation she was my wife. Although the outcome was beautiful and our story impacts lives daily, I would prefer that your story differ from mine.

One of the strongest desires of men is to express ourselves sexually. The challenge that comes with this is the level of access to so many illegitimate avenues of appeasing this desire. Whether it be pornography, masturbation, or just sharing yourself with multiple women, none of these choices are the smartest or healthiest for you. The bible defines our bodies as *temples and dwelling places of the holy spirit.* With these titles come the responsibility of taking care of and protecting our bodies at all costs. This includes abstaining from sex. Because of how normalized sex is, to be in a relationship and not have sex baffles the average person. You're not called to be average. As men, our biggest challenge with being sexually abstinent is our perspective. We allow ourselves to focus more on what we will be losing and less on what we will be gaining. So, let's take a second and discuss the common rebuttals for sexual abstinence among men.

The most common rebuttal of men as it pertains to abstaining from sex is, "If I'm going to marry someone, then I need to test drive her first so that I can know what I'm getting." First things first, this is a disrespectful analogy to use towards women because you are using a car to symbolize them. A car is a liability that decreases in value once you drive it off the lot therefore, using this analogy to describe sex with a woman is wrong and we haven't even gotten into the truth that combats this perspective. To hold onto this perspective is an expression your lack of belief that God is who He says He is. This perspective says that I don't believe that God is my provider, I don't believe that God will grant me the desires of my heart and I don't believe that my favor is found in finding my wife. If you believed these promises of God were true, then you would have the perspective that the God you serve would not create a wife for you that can't fulfill all of your needs. Now rebuttal number two will take less time to combat because there is no rebuttal number two. The only issue that men have with sexual abstinence is wanting to know if this individual can please their sexual desires and when it comes down to it if God is who He says He is then the answer is "Yes."

So now, let's talk about the benefit of sexual abstinence. If you have experienced any level of success, then you recognize the impact that self-discipline has on it. It is impossible to experience success or obtain accolades if you cannot discipline yourself into doing what needs to be done for the long term. One of the largest benefits of sexual abstinence is the self-discipline it builds within you. Not only will this benefit your relationship, but also your career, your finances and every other area of your life. Everything in life is a domino effect; therefore, how you do anything will affect the result of everything.

When discussing sex, there are two primary perspectives. One is embodied by the common man and the other is embodied by a husband. These two perspectives are that one sees sex as entertainment and the others sees sex as an opportunity for intimacy. One is an immature perspective and the other is the mature perspective. The husband understands that the blessing of sex is more than just a release. It is an opportunity to become one with your wife and share an experience of every type of intimacy all at once. The biggest benefit to sexual abstinence goes beyond discipline and beyond experience. The biggest benefit of sexual abstinence is the opportunity to show God how much you love Him. In John 14:15, Jesus says, "If you love me, keep my commandments" or in other words "If you love me, submit to me." Being sexually abstinent expresses submission to the will of God for your life. Therefore, do it like your life and the blessings of your marriage depend on it; Because, they do.

Key Points:

- Your willingness to be sexually abstinent reflects your belief that God is who He says He is.

- How you do anything will affect the result of everything.

- Your Willingness to be sexually abstinent is an opportunity to show God how much you love Him.

Chapter 9:

"I Do" Too

A fool once told me that getting married was the key to overcoming the battles you face as a single person. That fool was *me*. Going into marriage, I was under the belief that by making a covenant with God and my wife, the demons I faced in private would instantly go away. I was wrong. When you are in front of your pastor, friends, and family members saying, "I do," whatever baggage and issues you have yet to deal with are saying "I do," too.

The issue I assumed would disappear when I got married was pornography and masturbation. I was under the belief these issues were directly related to lust and would be fulfilled upon becoming married. I believed that because I was making this covenant with my wife and we could now have guilt-free sex, my desire to engage in pornography and masturbation would disappear. What surprised me was that not only did marriage not take away this issue, but it actually enhanced it. When I imagined myself being married, I saw my wife and I sharing in physical intimacy every day multiple times a day. This brings up one of the major problems with pornography. It causes you to create unrealistic expectations for your partner. Your mind doesn't process the fact you are looking at actors who get paid for this form of entertainment. Therefore you process it as real and project that expectation on your spouse.

I was surprised a few months into marriage when I faced the same temptation I was battling while single. I found myself falling as I did when I was single, promising God I would stop, deleting my browser history, using private browsers and every other trick you could use to engage in pornography and not get caught. Because no one was talking about this issue, I assumed that by reading my Bible, going to church, praying, and fasting occasionally, I would win over this old habit. What I realized is this addiction was being more affected by what I wasn't doing compared to what I was.

As we all do when true change is on the brink, I reached a point of being so frustrated that I went to God in prayer with an aggressive tone and disappointment. The result of the conversation was a revelation I use to help people gain freedom from many issues. The revelation that God gave was that, "demons thrive in darkness." He explained that the reason this issue was dominating my life was because of me hiding it due to the shame it was paired with. He informed me that hiding my issue was putting the demon in the environment that it was birthed in, therefore if I truly want freedom I have to shine light on the situation by talking about it. Whatever experiences or struggles that are present in your life are being given the power to thrive through shame. Your freedom from your issues lie in truth and seeking God for the wisdom to fully free yourself from this battle.

I would be remised to express the importance of dealing with your struggles if I didn't provide you with tangible steps of doing so. To overcome any challenge or struggle, there are seven steps that could be taken to completely alter the situation. The first step Is "surrendering the situation to God." With God being the all-powerful creator of all things, it would be in your best interest to lay your burdens down before Him and submit to the direction He provides. The second step is to, "bring your struggle to light." Having a brotherhood or sisterhood in place is critical for all people especially with accountability. With whatever your challenge may be, a large part of your freedom is having the ability share your truth with someone else. The third step in this process is to, "grow in understanding." Until you clearly understand why you shouldn't do what you are doing, you won't fully decide to stop doing it. Step number four in this process is to "Make yourself aware of who deserves your freedom." Your freedom from struggles not only benefit you, but also your family, friends and all of the individuals that God has called you to impact. Step number five is to, "recognize the pattern." There is a quote that says, "success leaves clues." I am a firm believer in this truth, but also the equal opposite of, "failure leaves clues." If you have been in a constant cycle of falling into the same sin it is very likely that the way you keep falling is the same. By you recognizing the pattern that leads to you falling into your sin, then you can become aware when you are in the pattern and disrupt it. The next step in the process is to, "Be cautious of your environment." Sin is always fueled by what you allow your senses to be exposed to, therefore if you desire to break free everything needs to go through the filter system of Philippians 4:8. The last and final step is to "set and go after goals." With everything that you are called to do the only reason you spend time choosing sin is because you have no plan in place to achieve what you are called to. By you setting

S.M.A.R.T goals and creating a plan to obtain them you won't have time to choose sin.

Lessons:

- When you say, "I Do," the challenges you struggle with say "I Do," too.
- Success and Failure leave clues.
- 7 Steps to freedom

Chapter 10:

The Fall Of Man

In June of 2018, my company at the time sent me to Beijing, China to do some work with our product team. During my first couple of days I experienced new levels of loneliness and disconnect. Following these feelings was the voice of God saying, "The way that you feel physically, mentally and emotionally is exactly where you have positioned yourself spiritually." Upon receiving this revelation, I repented for my lack of obedience and elevated my pursuit after God. One day as I was in my room doing some work, God gave me a message that was initially very random to me. God told me, "The reason relationships have not been succeeding is that they lack authentic transparency due to fear." The fear He was referring to is the fear of experiencing true love. Now everyone desires love which makes this message sound a little false, but the analogy He provided gave me true clarity about what He meant.

He directed my attention to the events in the Garden of Eden. When people discuss the fall of man, they focus primarily on Adam and Eve eating the fruit and less on what happens next. Following Adam and Eve taking a bite of the fruit that God forbade them to eat from, they then hid, which was the actual problem. Adam and Eve hiding from God created the same issue expressed in Mark 6:1-6. These verses discuss how Jesus went back to His hometown and could not do many works due to their unbelief. The unbelief of Adam and Eve after eating the fruit put God in a position in which He would not be fully active due to their lack of belief. Think about it. God created all things through words therefore if He wanted the fall to be reversed, He could just speak it. But because we were provided with free will, God was forced to let the fall happen due to the level of active unbelief they embodied. The moral of this revelation was that God created marriage to reflect the transparency and nakedness embodied by Adam and Eve in the garden with God before eating the fruit.

Now let's bring this back to marriage. As people, we all make mistakes and have skeletons in our past we prefer to keep hidden. Because of the shame towards these experiences we lock them in a closet, put up caution tape, dig a hole 30ft deep, drop the closet in the hole and build a church on top. We believe that it is in our best interest to hoarder the shame towards our experiences and think that it will not affect our future. Let me give you some advice I discovered the hard way. Wounds love attention and they will express themselves in every way possible to get it.

To truly experience love, you have to give someone the opportunity to fully choose you by providing them every reason not to. I tell people all the time that the reason I know my wife loves me is because she knows every bad thing I've ever done and still she wants to be here. To reach a place of having the tough conversation of transparency you have to go deeper in your belief in the identity given to you by Christ. As you go deeper into your identity, God will reveal to you who you are and kill the false beliefs that the enemy defines you with.

Lessons:

- The fall of man had more to do with lack of belief than eating fruit.
- Wounds love attention and will express themselves in every way possible to get it.
- True love is about giving someone every reason not to and them still choosing you.

A Mission For Marriage

As a couple, God has given my wife and I the responsibility of being the example of marriage and training people to walk out the journey of marriage how He designed it. This mission is fueled by the fact that neither of us grew up being provided with an example of what the proper marriage looked like. We were truthfully given every example of how not to do it and the responsibility of taking that information and using it to align ourselves. This alignment process was defined by the pain of trial and error, heartbreak and dysfunctional relationships. By experiencing the effects of being in and growing up around negative relationships, equipping individuals to be proper expressions of the true image of relationships will cure a lot of the pain we see in this world. We have said, "yes," to the calling of being the example and creating a new legacy for the generations to come and everything we create plays a role in doing so.

Be encouraged, my brother. You may not have grown up in the best environment or have been provided the best examples, but you are the best man for the job of changing your generational legacy. You are the best man for the job of showing friends and family members that healthy and thriving marriages are possible. You are the best man for the job to experience marriage as the reflection of Christ and His church and finally, you are the best man for the job of taking this information and sharing it with someone else.

References

https://www.biblegateway.com/passage/?-search=Ephesians+5%3A21-33&version=NIV

References:

https://www.biblegateway.com/passage/?-search=Ephesians+5%3A21-33&version=NIV

https://www.google.com/search?safe=active&rlz=1C1CHBD_enU-S795US795&ei=KRchXM3ZA8mgtQX-VpLzwDQ&q=submit&oq=submit&gs_l=psy-ab.3..0i67l4j0l6.98930.104855..105168...1.0..0.381.1828.0j2j0j4......0....1..gws-wiz.......0i71j0i131j35i39j0i131i67._BQQjM2ATb-M#dobs=submissive